SHAPELY

SELECTED FORMAL POEMS

by
JACK VEASEY

The Poet's Press

PITTSBURGH, PA

All poems © 2013 by Jack Veasey
All rights reserved
Second printing 2017

Poems in this volume have appeared previously
in the following places:

Literary Magazines:
Christopher Street, Experimental Forest, Fledgling Rag,
Fox Chase Review. The Horror Zine, Insight, Philadelphia Poets,
and *Wild Onions*

Chapbooks:
The Moon In The Nest, The Sonnets, 5 7 5

On The Web:
Sonnet Central; Sun Through A Broken Window

ISBN 0-922558-73-6
Also available as a PDF ebook

This is the 206th publication of
THE POET'S PRESS
2209 Murray Avenue #3
Pittsburgh, PA 15217

PRAISE FOR JACK VEASEY'S EARLIER BOOKS

One never wants to stop reading the kind of poetry Jack Veasey writes. There is, in joyous abundance, a diner where the likes of Whitman, Sandburg and Steinbeck could enjoy a cup of java. The spotlight of Veasey's work is humanity without varnish, without capped teeth and colored contact lenses. This is the apotheosis of the poetry of involvement. — Bob Tramonte, *Home Planet News*, New York City

The presumption in these poems that people have strengths that can carry them through hard times blends respect and admiration into an empathy for lives. The poem develops an awareness of humanity incarnate in the individual... Although I'm quite certain he is able to identify the tyrants around us, Veasey is not interested in casting out devils as much as he is in applauding the saints, those qualities of being human that are never so much lost as they are temporarily forgotten. — Frank Correnti, *The Pittsburgh Quarterly*

Whether his subject is a man living out of a bus station locker or a wide-eyed kid at a neighborhood fire, Veasey puts together blunt, cutting narratives that make you wonder how we can possibly accept things as they are. — Mike Gunderloy, *FactSheet Five*, Rensselaer, NY

His strongest poems are spare, sympathetic portraits that reveal whole histories of loneliness in small details. These are deceptively simple, surprisingly resonant poems. — David A. Warner, *The Philadelphia City Paper*

Many of his poems present an often troubling world where, for instance, people are relieved that a screaming siren near Three Mile Island signals the burning of a neighbor's house and not a nuclear meltdown, and where, too, the struggle to remain aware is a difficult one for those ground down by work . . . It is in his unresolved attraction to the outsider, his sense of being the only one, the other one, that Veasey shows the sensibility of all minorities. — David Eberly, *Bay Windows*, Boston, MA

The pen of a skilled poet can spin a solitary filament of words that snags readers and then expands to connect them with the writer and one another in a web of universal human emotions and experiences. Jack Veasey is that kind of poet . . . In plain talk that is simultaneously lyrical and lucid, Veasey writes of playgrounds and childhood, of the deaths of parents, of love and disappointment, of the price of forgiveness . . . simple but immensely effective. — Mary O. Bradley, *The Harrisburg Patriot-News*, Harrisburg, PA

The author is Irish and a lapsed Catholic. His background is blue-collar Philadelphia. His politics are anti- bureaucratic. But Jack Veasey's poems pack the appeal — and sting — of universality. . . Veasey speaks with the clarity and directness of an Everyman. . . a passionate poet of the people. — Jim Ruth, *Sunday News*, Lancaster, PA

ALSO BY JACK VEASEY

Handful of Hair (1975)
The Truth of Blue (1983)
Tourist Season (1984)
No Time for Miracles (1989)
Quitting Time (1991)
Down and Back (1993)
Tennis With Baseball Bats (1995)
The Moon in the Nest (2002)
The Sonnets (2007)
5-7-5 (2007)

TABLE OF CONTENTS

AN ASSORTMENT OF FORMS
Red Eye   13
Ways of Life   14
Desk Job   15
Consumed   17
The Saga of Bob   19
A Holiday   21
Panther   22
Control: A Rationale   23
Hunger for Things Not Canned   24
Do Not Go Gentle, Just *Go*   25
Real Man Rondeau   26
Rumination   27
Things We Forget   29
Jaded: A Salute to the 1970s   30
Compelled   31
"It"   32
Men's Room Senryu   33
Survivor Story   34
Sparring Partners   35
Same Name, Different Planets   36
X and Y   37
Kinetic   39
The Bloodhound Spell   41
Carousel   43
Neighbors   45
Ballad of the Morning After   46
Turnabout   48
A Blind Date with Phil Spector   49
Apocalypse   50
Spirit Anthem (Hymn Lyrics)   51
And Then Time Moves   52
Fathers and Sons   54
Visiting Hours   55
Widow's Hill   56
A Last Toast to Poe   57
Sorry, Emily Dickinson   58
Writes of Passage   60
A Deep Experience in Shallow Water   61
Winter Insight   62

SONNETS

Birth of Frankenstein   65
A Quiet Memory   66
Fear of the Dark   67
From Puberty to Poetry   68
Locker   69
Slur   70
Hypocrite   71
Defensiveness   72
Paranoia   73
On Reflection   74
Forgiveness   75
Physical Therapy   76
When I Met Gwendolyn Brooks   77
Epitaph for Quentin   78
Untitled   79
The Affair (A Crown of Sonnets)   80
Support   84
Child Beauty Queen   85
Moonlit Retreat   86
Young Nun   87
Exotic Dancer   88
Final Girl   89
Michelle's Truth   90
The Prince of Insomnia   91
Sobriety   92
A Sonnet to Smoke   93
Carnival   94
The Hoarders   95
The Legacy   96
The Spell of the Ruins   97
The Surrealists   98
Tookie   99
Friendly With Death   100
Dead Silence   101
Something Sensed on Samhain   102
A Shopping Mall Santa's Christmas Eve   103
Unresolved   104

The First Symptoms of the New Year   105
Varieties of Danger   106
Wild Rabbits   107
Hunter   108
Scarecrow   109
Purrogative   110
Toward Twilight   111
Night Blooming   112
The Green Man   113
Japanese Sonnet   114
Yes, Whitman Wrote No Sonnets, But . . .   115

HAIKU & SENRYU
Haiku and Senryu   119

FIXED FORMS USED IN THIS BOOK   125
NOTES ON POEMS   126
ABOUT THE POET   130
ABOUT THIS BOOK   132

SHAPELY

This book is dedicated to my late friend, the great guitarist Jack McGann. In 1973, Jack told me that I "really should" write sonnets to learn my craft. Being eighteen at the time, I told Jack that he "really should" mind his own business. It took me eleven years to start to follow his advice. I wish he could be here to see the results.

AN ASSORTMENT OF FORMS

RED EYE

I guess I am a passenger
And life, a train, a hurtling blur
From which I see
What pots cold strangers sit and stir
That won't fill me.

I eat a plastic sandwich on
The car that's there, then passed and gone;
The cellophane,
A softer pane peeled back at dawn —
Meat dry and plain.

The land, seen through a window, flat —
But steep if it is where you're at —
Reminds me of
A neighborhood I fled when that
Place held no love.

We locate hope wherever warm
Appears to supersede the storm
That scares us cold.
Suddenly, hope changes its form,
Is bought and sold.

But having paid the fare, I trust
Some sense will tell me when I must
Grasp what I've brought,
Step onto unfamiliar dust,
Again get caught.

WAYS OF LIFE

For Lynn Loomis

Everybody starts from where they are.
No matter where you start, the goal seems just as far.
You walk your mile, you beat your different drum.
This is one trip where you won't take a car.

From somewhere underground comes an unnerving hum.
Everybody starts from where they are,
But finds there is no rule of thumb.
In total dark, you can't follow a star.

Some wonder what their way will be, and some
Just seem to know where they should go, or come.
Though everybody starts from where they are,
Some go to church, some close the bar.

Some pull the strings, and some prefer to strum.
No movement and no music are enough for some.
Some think they walk on water — some,
        through knee-deep tar.
But everybody starts from where they are.

DESK JOB

Fluorescent lights make everyone look ill,
And all are chained, though these chains can't be seen.
The hardest work is waiting, waiting till
The stroke of five disarms the time machine.

And all are chained, though these chains can't be seen;
Each link's a payment pressing to be made.
The stroke of five disarms the time machine,
But bills and bills and bills wait to be paid.

Each link's a payment pressing to be made,
Each moment mortgaged till some future moment comes.
Bills and bills and bills wait to be paid,
As — between computers — conversation hums.

Each moment mortgaged till some future moment comes,
More and more paperwork piled softly in the bin.
As — between computers — conversation hums,
Forbidden music mustn't complicate the din.

More and more paperwork piles softly in the bin,
In cubicles the gods insist must look the same.
Forbidden music mustn't complicate the din,
and no framed photos. Just a plate that says your name.

In cubicles the gods insist must look the same,
Where light that's natural must never penetrate,
Are no framed photos. Just a plate that says your name
And where your heart should be, a leaden paperweight.

Where light that's natural may never penetrate,
Year after year of furtive search will only find
Where your heart should be, a leaden paperweight,
And no song but the drone of the dulled mind.

Year after year of furtive search will only find
That what we see remains all that we will,
And no song but the drone of the dulled mind
Can ease the ache from all this sitting still.

What we see remains all that we will.
The hardest work is waiting, waiting till
Retirement blunts the ache from all this sitting still.
Fluorescent lights make everyone look ill.

CONSUMED

All the people in the mall seem drugged,
Nodding as they stroll while Muzak plays.
Cameras everywhere — the place is bugged.
What's to see but strangers in a daze?

June, the would-be model, wants spiked heels.
Bubba, licensed for the hunt, wants shells.
Cigarettes, coats made from baby seals ,
Clerks will ring up anything that sells.

Gus, the guard, will show the homeless out;
What we never see must not exist.
Garden hoses are on sale — the drought
Was on that evening news we missed.

Veterans collecting for their kind;
Jars want coins for this disease or that.
Stephen King can occupy your mind.
Better pick up litter for the cat.

What you buy must be de-magnetized,
So you won't set off the shrill alarm.
Rite Aid's got a nurse with glassy eyes
Primed to stick a flu shot in your arm.

Where they keep what has been rearranged,
So you might buy more by accident.
You're bewildered — everything has changed —
Wondering where all your money went.

Escalators crawling toward the sky;
There's just plastic where you look for glass;
Hesitating — something's in your eye —
Step aside; the crowd comes surging past.

Time to navigate the parking lot;
Getting dark – you hope you won't get mugged.
Was there any item you forgot?
All the people in the mall seem drugged.

THE SAGA OF BOB

There once was a fellow named Bob —
A bigot dressed up as a snob,
Who thought his religion the One hole had pigeoned,
And that playing God was his job.

Bob spoke of a fellow named Christ —
A great man who was born just twice —
Who said we must hate all we did not create,
And control what we fear and despise.

What Christ *really* said, Bob ignored —
A most contradictory Lord —
Like "Do unto others…" and "Judge not your brothers,"
For Bob chose to live by the sword.

So Bob in the mirror did look —
Then picked what he liked from The Book,
And said, "I'm in His image, so in this Earth scrimmage,
Whoever's not me is a schnook."

Bob treats his employees like slaves,
And then smiles and says, "Jesus saves."
Words like "coon" and "kike" are the language he'd like,
But in public, this grey suit behaves.

And Bob votes for those who would cut
Medicare, Welfare, and God knows what.
Those children unborn, to protect, he is sworn,
But the living ones can kiss his butt.

There's one daughter Bob will not see,
Who lives with her love in DC.
Bob finds it a strain that her lover's named Jane,
So he's cut his youngest child free.

Bob's wife, he suspects, has a man
With whom she breaks God's sixth command.
But Bob looks away, because on Judgment day,
His Shalt Nots in good stead shall stand.

For Bob, love's not real, but pretend —
To love, after all, you must bend —
And any real giving requires risky living,
And fear has been Bob's trusted friend.

So we have this fellow named Bob —
A sad man, a miserable slob.
But everything looks so much better in books,
And only his God hears him sob.

A HOLIDAY

We walk along the plaza in the sun.
I miss our pets, and hope I locked the door.
You can't escape, despite how far you run.

The ancient temple gleams. The Buddhist nun
Speaks English. Did my bet mention the score?
We walk along the plaza in the sun.

Each foreign man looks better than the one
Before him. Smiling, you call me a whore.
 You can't escape, despite how far you run.

My therapist prescribed this trip. Some fun
Might soften our sore spots galore.
We walk along the plaza in the sun.

You say I've always been the only one.
Guilt stings me as you talk, and talk some more.
You can't escape, despite how far you run.

Location can't unlink a chain begun
When one thing led to others long before.
We walk along the plaza in the sun.
You can't escape, despite how far you run.

PANTHER

The most beautiful animal there is
Would shred your face and never hesitate.
Behind bars, his green eyes still radiate
Contempt for you and your cold camera.

But black and sleek, his image must, and will,
Hang on your wall and haunt you, like a hate
That takes decades until it starts to chill.
You captured him, and yet, now, you are his.

CONTROL: A RATIONALE

So "normal's" how things are when no one grows
Out of their brother's hand-me-downs and ways.
Too much change — no, we can't have that, God knows.

A normal boy gets by at school. His clothes
And haircut suit the general tone these days.
So normal's how things are when no one grows

His hair too long, or paints his nails, or shows
An interest in stuff teachers call "a phase."
Too much change — no, we can't have that, God knows.

Some water's deep. You wet more than your toes,
Get sucked in, and become one of the strays.
So normal's how things are when no one goes

Far off the path, follows their untrained nose,
Ends up a headline in the birdcage trays.
Too much change can be dangerous, God knows.

Trust family. When in on you they close,
It's for your good, despite how it dismays.
So normal's how things are when no one grows.
Too much change — no, we can't have that, God knows.

HUNGER FOR THINGS NOT CANNED

The coddled cat is outdoors for the night,
Dancing the role of predator again.
Though, by day, she sleeps on easy sheets kept white,
The coddled cat is outdoors for the night.
The eyes that close when her chin's scratched just right
Are blazing now, hypnotic, piercing, when
The coddled cat is outdoors for the night,
Dancing the role of predator again.

DO NOT GO GENTLE, JUST GO

When I turn for real, I turn for good.
You want forgiveness? Hey, don't hold your breath.
Should I write this down? Perhaps I should.

I can't forget offenses that drew blood.
But, sometimes, I don't hold a grudge till death.
Still, when I turn for real, I turn for good.

Your words, you say, have been misunderstood.
From accidental wounds, scars are still left.
Should I write this down? Perhaps I should.

A blade can mark flesh like an old desk's wood.
And I read your initials in my chest.
When I turn for real, I turn for good.

You say you won't repeat this, but you could.
So don't volunteer me for the test.
Should I write this down? Perhaps I should.

Your tears hide in the shadow of your hood.
Yet, sans my friendship, you swear you're bereft.
But when I turn for real, I turn for good.
Should you back off now? You bet you should.

REAL MAN RONDEAU

A real man knows; that's why his smile is thin.
 He keeps his secrets wrapped in his thick skin.
You're kept an arm's length back, where you belong,
Though what he took from you has made him strong
Enough to fight you off and — he thinks — win.

A real man tells you that to feel's a sin.
He *feels* that way, of course, but can't begin
To recognize how his right might be wrong.
A real man knows

How gentleness can threaten, for he's been
Out saving face among men just like him:
Alone and lonely, singing the tough song
To keep the pace, and carry all that weight along.
But where to turn when all his walls come falling in,
No real man knows.

RUMINATION

I cast a shadow
In which you can see
The things I remember,
still following me.

I cast a shadow —
Don't follow too near;
You'll fall in, and live
In that dark atmosphere

Where every exclusion
And snub are replayed,
And each unsaid sarcasm
sharpens its blade

For when I can say
What I'm dying to say,
Though it looks to the world
Like I've just walked away.

I cast a shadow
The color of rage
That darkens and festers,
And rattles its cage.

Old moments of love
Seem less vivid to me
 So those, I revisit
With less frequency.

I cast a shadow
And stir it like stew,
And, hearing it simmer,
Give warning to you:

What clings behind us,
And what waits before —
One is a quicksand pit,
One is a door.

What lies between them,
We're fools to ignore;
Here where we stand,
There's enough to explore.

If it's good example
You're hoping to see —
Your own shadow's smoldering;
Let it go free.

THINGS WE FORGET

The soft touch of a calloused hand
The space that fills an empty room
The light inside the dirty man
The bird that glides above a tomb

The space that fills an empty room
The sweetness in an urge that stings
The bird that glides above a tomb
The thin air that supports his wings

The sweetness in an urge that stings
The angel trapped in each sad thief
The thin air that supports his wings
The death that comes as a relief

The angel trapped in each sad thief
The light inside the dirty man
The death that comes as a relief
The soft touch of a calloused hand

JADED: A SALUTE TO THE 1970s

Sewers full of alligators,
Smarmy TV commentators,
So much now there is no later —
Look! A guy dressed like Darth Vader!
So what? An impersonator.
Nothing will exhilarate her.

Bored, bored, bored,
With both the Devil and the Lord.
Drop the dildo; sheath the sword;
She's left nothing unexplored.
Not even Fame —
Remember What's-his-name?

No, of course, you don't believe her —
Which night was that with the Fever?
Dancing in a suit all white,
Powder kept us up all night.
Hypertension killed us all.
Cut the whining — have a ball.

Let's eat some instant food.
Let's snort an instant mood.
Let's let the babysitter watch the brood.
Let's put off sorrow
Till clock-punch tomorrow.

Dance me down my drunken corridor
Into that shadow. Gimme More! More! More!

COMPELLED

He wanders into corridors unmarked,
Not knowing where he's going in the dark;
His only guide, his own delirium;
Foreshadowing him, his own anxious hum.
The tune, at least, is largely improvised.
His destination glows, but is unwise.
He's driven, or drawn on, by emptiness,
Assuaging it without the least finesse —
And yes, with medicine that's poisonous.
Symptoms season him; oh, don't let us discuss
His feet testing the wet floor, bare and cold.
He may get lucky. He may not get old.

"IT"

He moves through dark rooms,
Feeling his way. He is cold.
The others hid well.
The game's no fun with no hope.
Rich houses leave him so lost.

There — someone snickered.
Always snobs betray themselves.
There's no self control.
Poverty sharpens the scent.
The role of hunter reddens.

One tap; the role's passed.
So And So The Third is "It."
He always thought so.
Poor Man's invisible now.
Now the roles fit the players.

The game makes you prey.
If you don't fit, you hunt.
But that turn can pass.
One touch contaminates you.
To win, keep silent, stay down.

Time runs out too fast.
If the hunter stays hungry,
The squirrels can laugh.
This house is made of dead trees.
Only the loser can move.

MEN'S ROOM SENRYU

Golden scent of piss
Everywhere porcelain gleams
Macho graffiti

Magic marker words
KEEP YOUR FAG EYES TO YOURSELF
This must be the place

Tin booth called a stall
With a hole drilled through the wall
Jagged edge   think twice

Under the zipper
Under the rugged façade
Smoldering in vain

Smell of loneliness
Mixed with disinfectant smell
Nobody is clean

No admission here
No means of future contact
All's anonymous

Softer felt tip words
Prophet in the wilderness
SILENCE EQUALS DEATH

Zip up   head home   dream
Names exchanged, and tenderness
Hug pillow in sleep

SURVIVOR STORY

And so we struck this bargain, in the dark,
That I'd be your companion now and then.
I'd share your fever, hear your secret talk,
And see how you diverged from other men —
At least the ones you most resembled when
You'd get behind the big wheel for a drive.
The problem is that when you're gone, my friend,
I have to talk about it to survive.

You're like some twin conjoined, who'll disembark
From the shared hip. The bond does not extend
To daylight hours. I stagger through the park,
Hole in my side like Christ — withdrawn, the hand
That promised it would staunch the blood and blend
Its long struggle to mine. Away you'd dive,
And I'd scramble to bandage the loose end.
 I have to talk about it to survive.

You're wounded just like me, but you pretend
You're just another drone, building the hive.
When you buzz off, I've got heat to expend.
I have to talk about it to survive.

SPARRING PARTNERS

On again, off again — that's how it is.
Or was. Or will be. Hard to miss
The light that open door lets out.
Harder to ignore the last dark bout
That holds me back from what I'd kiss.

Your view, you flick like a switch: bliss
One minute; then scared stiff of this;
Then I back off, and then you pout.
On again, off again,

Knowing the steps — embrace, dismiss
Each other, but the feeling dis-
Agrees to disappear. And doubt
turns our tired heads. The turnabout
betrays the sigh behind the hiss;
On again, off again.

SAME NAME, DIFFERENT PLANETS

When you were small, I was your father's bud;
We hung out all the time. I was around
More than your relatives. You knew the sound
Of my voice on the phone. I was not blood;

You never called me "uncle," but I would
Bring gifts for you. Monster movies, I found,
Held you rapt all afternoon; you rewound
"the good parts" to watch them again. You could

be quite funny, sometimes. One day, watching
"Nosferatu," you told company it
dated "from before people could speak."

Now that you're grown, your Dad reports the sting
He felt when you called me a "fag" at sit-
Down dinner, when my name came up — a leak

Of your new attitudes. You always knew
My story. I was never anything
But friend to you. But you've revised your view
Across great distance, not based on remembering.

Your family moved down South in your teens.
Your Dad and I remained in touch by phone.
Amazing how a young man's life careens
Through changes when he separates from home.

I wonder what you'd call me to my face.
You claim to be above hate based on race.
I know that my behavior's not to blame.
Ironic — we still share the same first name.

X AND Y

It horrifies you that I tell the truth
Because you look much better in a mask.
You've worn that mask since early in your youth.
It horrifies you that I tell the truth
When you'd prefer the gleaming photo booth,
And how it lets you look just as you ask.
It horrifies you that I tell the truth,
Because you look much better in a mask.

My view of you creates embarrassment,
Because I can't blur certain features out.
Your soul wears earrings. I see where you're bent.
My view of you creates embarrassment.
You wish you were a straight line, and you meant
To smirk, but all you managed was a pout.
My view of you creates embarrassment
Because I can't blur certain features out.

If only I were not born to describe.
If only I could learn to shut my mouth.
But then, I couldn't serve you the sweet bribe.
If only I were not born to describe,
To testify, to witness for the tribe.
But then I couldn't kiss you North and South.
If only I were not born to describe.
If only I could learn to shut my mouth.

You've moved along. I'm sure you miss my skills.
You couldn't stay and risk being exposed.
I take a sip, and swallow my nerve pills.
You've moved along. I'm sure you miss my skills;
I pleasured you. But talking, talking kills.
My mouth kept moving. So your door was closed.
You've moved along. I'm sure you miss my skills.
You couldn't stay and risk being exposed.

To see you now, I'd have to close my eyes.
But I'd still see you stripped of your disguise.

KINETIC

They call it "a wild talent,"
To flex the mind like a muscle.
It seems like no gift, just lent,

Or rented, since you can't control
It yet. It surges of its own
Volition, so it seems. Its full

Force frightens you. It could break bones,
You're sure, the way it slammed that door.
You don't will it — it acts alone.

Seizure. A spasm of a sort,
Buzz in your head, and then the blood
Flows from your nose. A blur distorts

Your vision, and the flash sets wood
On fire, or boils puddles nearby,
Or smashes windows out, and, could

You focus it, you might defy
Any oppressor. It chastens
You instead. You can't rely

On it, can't make it happen
On command, can't hurl it like
Some sort of secret weapon.

The phenomenon could strike
At any moment, at a friend
Or property. You take a hike

Away from people. You blend
Into wilderness. Beasts fear you,
Give you a wide berth, and you tend

To keep a distance between you
And other humans. It is wise,
Perhaps, but fairly painful, too.

You'd have to wear an everyday disguise
To not frighten away a retinue.
Danger's apparent in your eyes

THE BLOODHOUND SPELL

I wish I had a bottle of your sweat;
I'd open it each night to taste your smell.
I treasure all my photographs of you,
But need to keep the scent of you as well.

I'd wear it on a chain about my throat —
A chain too thick to break, a chain of gold —
To ease those times when you'd grow too remote,
Too mad with your own guilt, too hard to hold.

I would enchant the sweat so it would last,
And never lose strength or evaporate.
I'd cork it; shield it from the sun; the glass
Would be dark brown — no rays could penetrate.

I'd rub it on a candle, like an oil
And light that candle, murmuring your name —
And anywhere you were, you'd think of me,
And feel a longing you could not explain.

Contagious magic, fragmentary hope
Clutched in the breast of one who cannot sleep;
Though threatened with the fire or hangman's rope,
These remnants of you I would fiercely keep.

And, though emotion drove you off, in time
Your inner coin would show its other side.
And it would be my face that you saw shine —
You can't pocket the sun, can't run, can't hide.

For I'd call to an empty space in you
With room enough for so much echoing
That, though you held your ears, word would come
through. That word would be my name. You'd feel a sting

I wish I had a bottle of your sweat —
The sweat not of your labor, but of sex
But all I have are fading photographs,
And this temptation to attempt a hex.

CAROUSEL

Parents watching are a blur
Wooden horses rise and fall
Music blares from a machine
Brass rings beckon to the tall

Chariots fixed to a floor
Zebra, tiger, lion, pig
Saddles carved in wooden flesh
Rabbit hops but does not dig

Grip the pole pierced through the heart
Of the steed that never sweats
Will the runt grab any rings?
Flask-drunk Dads are making bets

You are grey yet you will ride
Unafraid to look the fool
Grabbing greedy at the rings
Not concerned with looking cool

I ride on the horse behind
No, I am not in pursuit
Close my eyes and see my mind
Hurtling down a darkened chute

Faded murals that we pass
Picture when we weren't born
No one finds the ride too fast
Young girl straddles unicorn

Stirrup dance, three quarter time
Brassy tune too stale to hum
When there was no fatal crime
Nothing beaten but a drum

Turning back and then away
Only half a ticket left
Flashbulb catch the flying day
Here and now there is no death

NEIGHBORS

He seemed so normal, all his neighbors say,
Although they'd only speak to say hello.
He'd jump your car or dig it out of snow,
Collect your mail when you'd be gone away.

He'd always greet you with a smile or wave.
There *was* that odd smell, which he said he'd fix.
Seemed he was trying, with cement and bricks,
At least to get that cellar dirt floor paved.
Who'd ever guess it held more than one grave?
We noticed how young men would come and go.
 We'd see them when they came, at any rate.
Poor, lean, and scruffy — wouldn't want to know
They'd touched your daughter, but if they'd work, great.

We wondered why they never seemed to last.
We figured they'd moved on for higher pay,
Or just to stay high, period, since they
Looked half baked half the time, and you'd smell grass.

The thing to do was not notice too much,
Although the wife was one to watch and talk.
OK, maybe the guy's just a soft touch
Who picks up strays, and, in a while, they walk.
Who ever dreamed we'd see outlines in chalk?

BALLAD OF THE MORNING AFTER

"Why were you out all night?" he asked.
"Your eyes and hair are wild."
"None of your business," she replied.
"Don't treat me like a child."

"You're only seventeen," he snapped.
"I ought to slap your face.
You're acting like a bitch," he said.
"Those clothes are a disgrace."

She went upstairs and slammed her door.
She locked it with the bolt.
He banged on it, called her a whore.
The word gave her a jolt.

You'd never understand, she thought.
She didn't know herself
What made her act the way she did.
She feared for her own health.

She pulled the scarf off of her neck.
She looked hard in the glass.
Two angry red holes took her back
Into the recent past.

But now it seemed more like a dream,
A soft blur in her mind —
A touch that made her faint
And left strange images behind.

Bright eyes like coins shone in the dark.
Her back was on cold grass.
Whatever drew her to the park
Caught her, and held her fast.

A funny feeling wouldn't let
Her talk about it now.
She'd choke on her words if she did;
She's sure of that somehow.

Someone would know, someone she feared,
Yet yearned to see again,
A face that stayed in shadow
Though so near her own. *Pretend*

It didn't happen, something told
Her now. *Lie down and get some rest.*
She did. She felt a weakness, and
A sharp pang in her chest.

When she awoke, her room was dark.
She must have slept all day.
Somebody at the window said,
Invite me in. It took her breath away.

TURNABOUT

The dark place opens when I close my eyes —
Your not-so-secret secret life exposed.
In games, the table-turner is surprise.

Your mean relations based the game on lies.
While you were hiding, they'd shred your best clothes.
The dark place opens when I close my eyes.

Whoever loves you most, you must despise,
Because the rules insist — though why, God knows.
In games, the table-turner is surprise.

You tell me all my actions are unwise.
To gloat's your only pleasure, I suppose.
The dark place opens when I close my eyes.

You don't expect it when affection dies
In those you've charmed, whose small joys you oppose.
In games, the table-turner is surprise.

Your beauty doesn't blind me now. The prize
Is all I see. The scar you gave me glows.
The dark place opens when I close my eyes.
In games, the table-turner is surprise.

A BLIND DATE WITH PHIL SPECTOR

Take one look at the guy, and run.
The wigs he wears are weird enough.
Pass up the deal; he waves a gun.

Though he has mansions, pools and stuff,
And jeweled rings that catch the sun,
Take one look at the guy, and run.

Unless your head is full of fluff,
Or you've lived sheltered as a nun,
Pass up the deal; he waves a gun.

A long life, whether rich or rough,
Is better than one too soon done.
Take one look at the guy, and run.

The songs may promise endless love
That stays the way it was begun.
Pass up the deal; he waves a gun.

Don't hang around to call his bluff.
He's not some saint who just talks tough.
Take one look at the guy, and run!
Pass up the deal; he waves a gun!

APOCALYPSE

The ultimate horror —
A spider with wings.
Mad doctor makes one,
And fat lady sings.
Which nation has it,
Will hand out the stings;
Their Nero is fiddling,
and tidings he brings;
Where there is smoke,
No one's safe, even kings,
And something *is* burning —
The fabric of things.

SPIRIT ANTHEM (Hymn Lyric)

The spirit may not have a name
Nor laws to live by to impose
And yet it fills this empty frame
With light the way rain fills a rose

The spirit may not raise us high
Above what strangers we might fear
Yet shake the hand, and meet the eye
And all mistrust may disappear

The spirit flows through us like blood
And we all bleed when wounds invade
The spirit makes flesh more than mud
When from our struggles bonds are made

The spirit lives in all and each
despite what differences we see
Don't turn away from what can teach
Diversity is unity

The spirit can be recognized
In every shade the rainbow holds
No one excluded or despised
Beneath this flag the sun unfolds

We find our path, we sing our song
Our faces open to the sky
We find the spirit is too strong
To be held down, or to deny

The spirit lives in all and each
despite what differences we see
Don't turn away from what can teach
Diversity is unity

...AND THEN TIME MOVES

The tattooed man struck her as ominous
When she first saw him naked. But his face,
Wet from the pool, seemed open as his hands.
She scanned him for that quality that glows
From inside, and believed it there. His blue
Eyes didn't hurt. She watched close for what moves.

Beauty seems a firm first basis, and moves
Us in lieu of facts. Some call this ominous.
Nonetheless, her mood would shift the lights to blue
If she should pass a day without his face
Turned to hers. Anything that hums and glows
Needs tending. Soon this duty filled his hands.

He'd always had some task to suit his hands,
But he was used to wood, not clay that moves.
He'd shape her in ways that, sometimes, glow
And sometimes throw a shadow, ominous.
He'd read few books, and could not read her face.
He'd babble with no clue till his turned blue.

Her righteousness bewildered him. Soon blue
Became the shade of all his days. His hands
Strayed to more pliant subjects. Soon his face
Spoke fluently to her, and she made moves
That anyone could read as ominous.
Still he was startled, flushed with rage that glows.

Some men can't see what, to some others, glows,
She found a substitute to light her blue
Flame, who bore a resemblance ominous
That she did not see. She fit in his hands.
Meanwhile, her "old man" wondered if his moves
Had failed him. With age, pain showed in his face.

Things occurred to him — hard for a man to face.
His inked skin was a warning sign that glows.
At his age, he could not count on old moves
That long ago could turn her music blue.
He had a problem in his empty hands.
The situation seemed quite ominous.

Ominous indeed. We see just the face
We first find in our hands. Eyes open, glow
Blue — we believe their light. And then time moves.

FATHERS AND SONS

Fathers and sons — what a subject.
Here to teach, learn from, love and protect
Each other, so some unseen "they"
Supposedly have said. But say
What you will — distance will inject

A dose of chronic discord to deflect
The word, the touch that might clearly project
The softer side most guys are frightened to betray.
Fathers and sons

Circle each other in the cages they erect,
Giving and taking only what you would expect
Of skillful sportsmen at serious play.
The stalemate won't become a truce until the day
Death comes for one, and makes one sad kiss perfect
For father and son.

VISITING HOURS

She wasn't up for visitors that day.
She lay face down in bed and cried and cried.
The last time I saw her, she sent me away.

What was wrong, I couldn't make her say,
No matter what the strategy I tried.
She wasn't up for visitors that day.

Supposedly retired from the fray,
Yet driven to march on, restless inside,
The last time I saw her, she sent me away.

Her fear of something blanched her features grey —
Something unseen and unidentified.
She wasn't up for visitors that day.

The reason why, her words would not betray,
But "I won't be here long," she prophesied.
The last time I saw her, she sent me away.

The Home was not her home; she couldn't stay.
Unable to rest there, she simply died.
She wasn't up for visitors that day.
The last time I saw her, my mother sent me away.

WIDOW'S HILL

The cemetery overlooks the sea.
The waves, not the white stones, go on forever.
What image lets us taste eternity?

Down drop the flowers, begging silently
To not go with the box when it goes under.
The cemetery overlooks the sea.

The priest intones with such solemnity
Such formal words, how can God not deliver?
What image lets us taste eternity?

The coffin lowers. The soul is set free,
So some believe — a darker view for others.
The cemetery overlooks the sea.

The mourners turn away, look longingly —
At waves crashing below the cliff — through tears.
What image lets us taste eternity?

A stone angel observes all neutrally.
Its face betrays no thought of what it hears.
The cemetery overlooks the sea.
What image lets us taste eternity?

A LAST TOAST TO POE

The cognac and the rose
Were left each year, God knows
By whom, to honor your birth.
Suddenly it stopped.
Perhaps the donor died.
Six decades had gone by
Since it began, your grave's turf
Yearly decorated,
Your ghost long vacated
From that narrow plot of earth.

SORRY, EMILY DICKINSON

Binoculars, kaleidoscopes,
And other vision toys,
Diminishing the distance
Between us and our joys;
What we see may be accurate,
But still it's out of reach —
Its closeness an illusion,
With lessons cold to teach.

A memory's a souvenir,
And so is every scar.
Though you're a map
Of where you've been,
You don't fit where you are.
You visualize strange continents,
And hope to see your soul —
Afraid to look inside yourself
And find a gaping hole.

Confusion talks itself into
A first attempt at Art,
And finds in indecision
Odd wisdom from the heart.
The poet in seclusion
may not see all that much —
but, if she babbles long enough,
she's bound to get in touch.

Some may not see the point of
So much talking to yourself;
Though you do it on paper,
And store it on a shelf.
At best, you're an eccentric;
At worst, you're called insane —
Until History validates
The contents of your brain.

You long for recognition;
You send out through the mail
Your mind's peculiar images,
Your heart pierced by a nail.
You get a stuffy answer
Spawned by a stuffy head —
Professors just won't catch your drift
Till after you're long dead.

WRITES OF PASSAGE

What comes to mind
When hand meets pen,
And eye meets page,
And time subsides —
Or so it seems?
We fill the reams
From our insides —
Our cup of rage,
Our endless yen
To break the bind.
But we are blind,
We hungry men —
Testing the cage,
Making small strides
Despite big dreams.
The last word beams
Beyond long rides
To the next stage,
The next, and then —
What's left behind?

.

A DEEP EXPERIENCE
IN SHALLOW WATER

A little island in the river, just
Before the railroad bridge — you spread a towel
There to "lay out" that sunny day. We must
Both be there, you said; maybe you'd allow

Me to go swimming. Those who go alone can
Drown. Our river was so shallow, I just laughed
At that. When you rolled on your belly, and
My book got dull, I waded ten yards off

To find the small sand beach where raccoon hands
Left their impressions. I was nearly there
When I tripped on a rock, tipped sideways and
Fell to the bottom of a cold pool where

The current swirled, and held me down. Two feet
Deep is deep enough to cover a man's
Face. I lay there on my side, a complete
Exile, like a fish who'd flopped out on dry land,

Only my element was air. I fought
To rise, despite surprisingly strong force.
Gasping, at last I popped up like a thought
Unwelcome; of that, there'd been no "of course."

I staggered on land near your sunning place.
You lay still stomach down; your hidden face
Had never looked my way while I was gone.
Only the river had caught me alone.

WINTER INSIGHT

A fly on the lip of the glass,
A drink that the room has turned cold;
There's some contradiction in this.
This season indoors breaks the mold.

You take an intoxicant sip
Of brew grown belatedly strong.
You let the nip soothe your cold throat
And find your voice, but not for long.

The drunken fly's small life expires.
The flush in your skin will not last.
You sing about seasonal fires
And stay inside, dreaming the past.

The summer to come is far off;
The previous one, just a blur.
Your song terminates in a cough,
And you feel worse off than you were.

You know no other moment will provide
Relief that — though you can't reach it — you crave.
It's more than a dark lull in the year's ride.
This quick flash of the wings is all we have.

SONNETS

BIRTH OF FRANKENSTEIN

Lightning awakened me. I was strapped down.
In many places, I felt stitches itch.
I smelled of brimstone. Every muscle twitched.
The cry, triumphant, "IT'S ALIVE!" soon drowned

In thunder, a few steps behind the flash.
Then his face looking down at me, wild-eyed
And sweaty. Handsome, though. I heard a sigh
Emerge from me. He smudged this thumb with ash,

Drew something on my forehead. This was my
Mark of the unbaptised; though my life spark
Came from God's sky, my sky was cold and dark.
My future would hold only misery.

I was not his child, but his creation.
Product disappoints imagination.

A QUIET MEMORY

We rode bikes on the boardwalk, Dad and I,
On early mornings, while the crowd still slept.
We shared the time much like a secret kept —
That truce was possible. It was a guy
Thing, one might say, not mentioning that Mom
Was not in sight. Well, not in hearing was
More to the point. Gulls only broke the calm —
Gulls and the softly crashing tide, because
Mom wasn't here, could fill our ears with round,
Warm tones. Even the wheels were mute — no card;
No squeak; just turning without sound.
To go long without talking was not hard.
There was no need for any other noise.
There could be peace out there, for just us boys.

FEAR OF THE DARK

There is a monster underneath the bed
of every toddler on a stormy night
when clouds collide and flash an awful light
unlike the sun's, and bang to wake the dead.

The monster flails its slimy tentacles
As if to snatch any uncovered limb
That hangs unblanketed, thus tempting him
To drag the whole child down to where he dwells.

All kids know this, and all parents dismiss
The whole idea that monsters can exist.
They don't see how a monster in the head
Is clearer than the one under the bed.

And so we hide our heads, imagining
That our dear parents don't know everything.

FROM PUBERTY TO POETRY

Because I was a gawky kind of guy,
With thick bifocals and burgeoning zits;
Because my laughter was a tone too high,
And I, a size that no known clothing fits;
Because the music I loved wasn't cool,
Much like the books I read, and things I said;
Because we were all kids, and kids are cruel,
And, if you don't exactly fit, you're dead —
I didn't rise to top the class like cream;
I didn't study and apply myself;
I didn't even try to make the team,
Or pave my way for future ease and wealth.
I cherished all they pressured me to hide —
And refused to prove them right by suicide.

LOCKER

It was the only private place in school —
Regrettably, too small to crawl inside.
The padlock meant you had some space to hide
What private stuff you'd dare keep in a cruel

Environment: the face for which you were a fool,
Taped to the door; a notebook where you lied
In secret to yourself; the knots you tied
Trying to cast some sort of spell, which you'd

Believe in if it worked. You'd go at times
When no one came nearby, no one could see
To laugh at, or describe, your hidden things.

You'll live through this and look back. Drinks with limes
Will make you laugh at this dull memory.
You tell yourself that now, while the name stings.

SLUR

No, this is not a superficial wound,
Although not one that anyone could see;
No salve can soothe, no bandage can entomb
An ache from which no pill can set you free.
Remembering the moment of attack,
You flinch again, recoiling from the blow;
That voice again, that sneering voice comes back,
And all your best defenses are too slow.
The weapon left its mark — you feel it still,
Although its tracks are not blue, black, or red.
The moment's passed, but now you walk uphill,
With every step a new throb in your head.
The wound feels deep, although it seems absurd —
Although made by no knife, but by a word.

HYPOCRITE

You claim to follow Jesus, yet you hate;
He told you not to judge, lest you be judged;
Though He said, "do unto others," you berate
Whoever's presence unnerves you. No nudge

Is needed to make you turn uglier.
You seethe if there's the slightest hint
That someone's crossed the rigid barrier
Erected during your unpleasant stint

In child form, or by something Daddy said,
Or pulpit platitudes Mom parroted.
You'll always be the first to throw that stone,
Spit in that eye despite planks in your own.

You say there is no other way to live,
And every day do harm others forgive.

DEFENSIVENESS

This is a glass pane shattered by a fist,
Through which invading wind can surge unscathed;
This is the green tattoo that shouts, RESIST,
But brands the man who wears the word a slave.
This is the size of fear, the shape of hate,
The voice of silence that denies them both —
We build a higher wall and bar the gate,
But, nonetheless, realities encroach.
There is no place to hide from what we feel,
No mask our shaded gaze can't recognize.
The seeds we bury fester, then congeal,
Then bear their bitter fruit before our eyes.
This is the secret everyone can see
Too late; *that* is the final irony.

PARANOIA

No, I don't live in fear; fear lives in me.
It follows me around and dogs my days.
What triggers it, I may not hear or see,
But my imagination has its ways.
A stranger's glance misread, a laugh nearby,
No conversation heard — just tones of voice;
Convinced the subject's me, moved to reply,
I make enemies as if I have no choice.
A dying bee on autumn's windowsill —
No strength to sting, it flounders in the cold.
Afraid, I raise my newspaper to kill
This creature that already won't grow old.
That fluttering on the periphery
Must be a threat; I take it personally.

ON REFLECTION

A young man who admired the distant past
Perused a book he'd found under some dust.
He knew the light around him wouldn't last.
He knew what he could touch, he couldn't trust.
He looked among the shadows and the mist
For faded faces he might recognize,
For obstinate old legends that persist
For generations, though the story lies.
Truth, yellowed, crumbled at his fingertips,
Long paled beside what he'd learned to believe.
He read aloud. What passed between his lips
Described things that he'd never seen, yet grieved.
He was the keeper of a doorless key.
Years later, he is still hidden in me.

FORGIVENESS

Forgiveness is a scarce commodity,
The price of which goes up year after year.
It's given, but not handed out for free;
Both giver and receiver pay, I fear.
We mustn't only listen, we must hear;
Both sides must be clear to each other's eye.
The price is truth's pain, and the price is dear;
And, sadder still, there is no price too high.
And so we strike dark bargains, by and by;
We struggle down the road to compromise;
Agree to bend, accept each flaw, and try
To cut our own needs down to size;
We put each other's shoes on for awhile.
We made the error; now we face the trial.

PHYSICAL THERAPY

In pain, the damaged gather here to heal —
Our progress slow, unlike a miracle.
Machines don't hear our prayers, but the pull
And push and stretch that they demand make real

The missing balance muscle needs to feel.
You work on where you're weakest. Pain turns dull
As months inch by, your weekly schedule full
Of visits here, where rubber, rope and steel

Resist you. But your body moves along.
The clanking plays a hidden melody.
The change may not be one that you can see

But, rising from a chair now, nothing's wrong.
The inner stab you used to feel is gone.
The work's reward comes — just not suddenly.

WHEN I MET GWENDOLYN BROOKS

My job was to help her sell her books.
I sat beside her at the folding table.
I made change while she met admiring looks
And signed her name as much as she was able.

Where I sat intruded on her aura.
It wouldn't work if I'd sat far away.
Somebody'd brought a huge bouquet of flora,
Which someone else had quickly whisked away.

No room here for anything but books. She
Signed mine, "To My Colleague" — what a thrill!
The line was long. I thought, perhaps, that we

Might chat when it was over. But until
The place was closing, she was occupied.
I'm honored she brushed by me in her stride.

EPITAPH FOR QUENTIN

*Charisma is the ability to influence without
the use of logic.* — Quentin Crisp

Quentin was a very gentle man.
His voice and hands were soft; his hair was white
With streaks of pink dyed in. There was a light
Around him that protected him from hands

That meant him harm, although he'd have denied
Such things could be. Every man was "Mister"
To him, every woman "Miss" or "Mrs."
There was more to him than manners — he tried,

Though, to embody etiquette. Feelings,
He would say, are just a luxury one
Can't afford, at least beyond a certain
Age. Yet his highest art was sparing them.

He lived in one room that he never swept.
When he passed from us, even the dust wept.

UNTITLED

You still don't know, and I won't tell yet. I
Will revel in the innocence of this.
What you don't know won't hurt me, and the bliss
Of which I'm ignorant is best a sigh

Left lingering where longings hide, within
Fond fantasy, the place where longings live
The longest. I look on you as mystics in
The state of grace see God's face, God's forgive-

Ness; your skin, gleaming beyond reaching. But
I know, from what you've told me, of your wound
within — deep, much like mine, the troubling cut
made on your mind when tyrants called your tune.

We have both been laughed at, left out, lost and poor.
But of this bond between us, I am still not sure.

(first attempt at a sonnet, 1984)

THE AFFAIR (A CROWN OF SONNETS)

We were attached; you knew, but you denied
That I could be the end of your long search.
But as for me, I knew I was in church,
Or thought I did. I knelt, discarding pride
And dignity and old beliefs. I tried;
In all my years of sad, frantic research,
I hadn't found a way to feel allied;
Even my parents left me in the lurch.
You had a family, a hiding place
Where you could feel — if somewhat fettered — safe.
You had a past you wanted to forget,
And longings you ached with, but couldn't face.
We knew each other at first sight, yet gave
In slowly — helpless, and with some regret.

Slow, helplessly, our fear and our regret
Proved too weak to hold back what felt so strong.
You burned for what I'd give, but thought it wrong.
Or so you said. Yet, soon after, you let
Me do the things you'd always wanted. *Get
While you can, love who you're with,* some song
From your wild past led you this far along,
Perhaps, and I became your drooling pet.
I loved you like a dog, expecting just
A fond stroke in return, a sometime walk,
A bone or table crumbs; I'd beg for those.
I felt, if long unused by you, I'd rust,
And you seemed happy your new tool could talk.
You told me hidden things — true, I suppose.

You told me hidden things – true, I suppose,
Of young days when you broke the law for fun,
Of women and men conquered on the run,
And how much you'd been loved by some of those.
My lust grew with each secret you disclosed.
I felt blessed to be the next in line, un-
Done by your exciting life, your eyes that stun,
Your rambling voice, the smell of you so close.
My family had always let me down;
I didn't see why yours should feel betrayed.
I wasn't fazed by lies you'd tell another.
You were the man I couldn't be, a crown
Bright on your handsome head. And when we played,
This only child was suddenly called brother.

This only child was suddenly called brother,
Euphemism though it was. I became
Your sidekick, like in buddy films; no blame
Followed me here from childhood streets. *Smother
The past*, I thought. *God, at last, another
Chance.* I was a new man, I'd discover
Kingdoms other men had always known. Blur
That those days were, I couldn't see how tame
You'd quickly made me, how I'd shelved my needs
To gladly service yours. An act of love,
it was for me; you wanted just a ball.
Guard down, I'd blurt the wrong words, and the seeds
They planted bore new fear in you. Above
All else, this had to stay a game you'd call.

Because this had to stay a game you'd call,
You made up rules that I'd already bent.
You put me through a period like Lent;
Each time I'd ask to see you, you would stall.
The weeks dragged by; I feared, too, now, that all
Would turn to nothing, that you would invent
A stronger rationale for time unspent
Together, for "practical reasons." Wall
After wall was thrown up, sure enough. You
Said weeknights *and* weekends were bad, gave
No hope, only unending puttings-off.
Though none of it rang anything like true,
You said, "Don't take it personally." *Be brave*,
I told myself, until I'd had enough.

I told myself, until I'd had enough,
That what shone in your eyes belied your words.
It was your love, not mine, that had incurred
This act that you put on of talking tough.
You spoke to me of friendship — all that stuff
About how you "liked me a lot," and hurt
Was not what you intended. A bird
In your chest fluttered, felt the cage; wings shoved
Against cold metal bars that would not yield.
It didn't matter much how bad I felt —
You'd say one thing, but cling to your own way.
My anguish could no longer be concealed,
And time dragged on. I watched what I'd built melt.
I, too, was family you could betray.

I, too, was family you could betray.
Close, yes, but never close enough to break
Through that last wall of coldness, maybe shake
You up enough that you'd cave in and pay
The price for what you stole. But you'd just say
You cared, then act as if you didn't. Take,
You'd do with relish, but make no mistake —
You wouldn't give an inch to save my day.
Your actions didn't speak of any care,
Although you knew my pain was deep — it seems
On love repressed, not much can be relied.
No loss would draw it out, no tears, no screams.
We were attached; you knew, but you denied.

SUPPORT

You sit with me before my surgery
And stroke my hand, and softly lend support;
Awhile without a word, yet you report
A wealth of subtle sentiments to me.
The nurse pops in, and says that the I.V.
May pinch me; I don't let my face contort,
Wanting to seem brave and polite. We court
The best blood pressure with infused tranquility.

It's time to go. The doctor shakes your hand
As if we're at a sports event. I say
"I love you," as you do, with confidence.

They wheel me off. Though I wear no gold band,
I feel your presence near me when I fade.
I'll wake wrapped in your silent eloquence.
.

CHILD BEAUTY QUEEN

Tiffany's nine. Her hair extends her height
By half a foot, piled high in sculpted curls.
Her eyes seem huge. False lashes and blue lids
Enhance the luminous come-hither look
Disturbing from a face so young. Hands on
Her hips, she poses like a stripper, as
The lights gleam on her smile — elaborate
Dental work replacing baby teeth with
False. Her fingernails are long and painted.

Her dress? Red as a flashed-on neon sign,
Low cut, though there are no breasts yet to see,
And short enough to show most of her legs,
In fishnet stockings (also red). The crowd
Applauds. Her mother wishes rivals dead.

MOONLIT RETREAT

She walked into the water silently,
Long after sunset briefly turned it red.
She stopped before the black murk reached her head
And stood neck-deep, embraced, but so coldly.

The lake had been her friend since she was small.
More faithful than most humans, it had proved.
It startled her a bit when something moved
Across her shin. But she was safe. A call,

Perhaps an owl's, reminded her to breathe.
She hadn't known where else to go to hide.
Her father wouldn't find her here. He'd tried
Again. She felt that no one would believe

Her if she told. She kept it clenched inside.
She'd swim across, but thought the lake too wide.

YOUNG NUN

She wears all black, although the weather's warm.
Her clothes conceal what curves defined her form.
A ceremony took a man's first name
And grafted it to her, so when there came

A visitor, she'd seem even more strange.
She knows there is a point to all this change,
But sometimes, now, she wonders who she is.
The girl is gone. Her mother calls her "Liz"

And it seems odd. It doesn't fit her
Anymore, like these clothes half a size too
Large. She fingers beads like vertebrae

And counts them too, to keep track of her prayer.
How many repetitions must she do,
Like lifting weights, until she fills her day?

EXOTIC DANCER

She dances on a pole to pay for school.
She'll tell that to a guy who comes too close.
She's nervous with the ones who get verbose.
Her body has a price; grab at her soul,

And she'll just slap your hand away. The rule
Is hers: external friction only goes
So far for tips. No man can say he knows
Her mind; none of them even know her major. Roll

With the punches, when life gives you lemons,
Etcetera; she might say those. The tunes
Throb through her body — that much, she will feel.

She'll show the whole shebang. That part is fun;
Defying the forbiddings, toss a moon
Out a bus window. Her real name, she won't reveal.

FINAL GIRL

The killer will not get around to her
Until his winning streak runs out of steam.
The carcasses in which her friend's souls were
She'll stumble on – no, no, it's not a dream.

A wound will wake her up. She'll start to run.
She won't care about who the killer is.
No, *what* he is, and how he has his fun,
Now drive her actions just as hard as his.

She'll scan each room she hurtles through to find
Whatever weapon-like objects may lie
Within quick reach. She has virginity
On her side, though no morals cross her mind.

To live, at all, pre-empts questions of how,
As her running time nears its ending now.

MICHELLE'S TRUTH

The last time I was in the hospital,
I was in group with this girl named Michelle.
Bandages were on her wrists, and she'd tell
Us how she cut herself "to let the pain out.," all

The while picking exposed scabs further up.
Something about her haunted me. She made
An awful kind of sense. I'd never had
The urge myself, yet I felt soon I'd pop

Like a balloon, full of old pressures I'd
Inhaled, held in — just couldn't let them go.
Maybe this girl knew what I didn't know.
My pulse was throbbing like a dammed-up tide.

That pounding drowns it out when docs explain
Dull facts — like blood is blood, and pain is pain.

THE PRICE OF INSOMNIA

I lay awake all night, then slept till three.
The damn Internet wouldn't let me on.
I'm still disoriented from my dreams,
And virus tricks prove all control is gone.

I can't get started, just like the used car.
I can't accomplish half of what I'd planned.
The screen drags me to ads for these bizarre
Appliances Mom wouldn't understand.

The mailbox fills with bills I can't afford.
My bowels repeatedly rush me upstairs.
The bank tells me card interest rates have soared.
Too bad the payment can't be made in prayers.

If going back to sleep would help, I'd try.
Last night, I couldn't. Hmm. I wonder why.

SOBRIETY

To keep it to myself — this flesh that aches
To brush against another's flesh too soon;
To keep from having that one drink it takes
To get me shouting curses at the moon;

To keep from loving anybody flawed,
Who might disrupt my precious peace of mind;
To keep my cool reserve from being thawed;
To keep from being caught, and left behind;

To keep from breathing in the world's foul germs,
And getting sick enough to need a cure;
To keep from feasting on dead meat like worms,
And keep my body tight and trim and pure;

To keep to this clean path — now that's ambitious!
If only it weren't quite so repetitious.

A SONNET TO SMOKE

Out in the cold, smoke clouds surround his head;
He's on the porch to spare his family.
So many smokers he has known are dead.
Now he exhales their ghosts reluctantly,

Savors gruff voices coming back to him,
Still rumbling low boasts and obscenities —
Such vivid figures once, now growing dim,
Fathers who left a fading legacy.

Unlike the trains on earth, the train to hell
Must surely have a smoking car. He smiles
At that thought — rueful, but it rings a bell.
The thought of smoking after sex beguiles

No more. Our customs change; we live and learn.
Well, some of us do. Others slowly burn.

CARNIVAL

Twice a year it comes to town, imported
By the local lodge. The grungy men who
Run the rides attract the girls who get led
Easily, just as the lights will draw bugs, too.

Boom-box music blares (calliopes are
Relics of the past). Men, they attract with
Wooden ducks that march in rows. A bright blur
Greets the drunken eye whose spirits get a lift

From a good gawk. Obnoxious local punks
May volunteer to hurl abuses at
The crowd, until one throws a ball and dunks
Him in a shallow tank. It's all old hat,

But in a town this small, what can compete
With rides, games, grunge, and greasy things to eat?

THE HOARDERS

Collected by us, objects multiply
As if they were blessed with fertility,
As if they copulated on the sly —
Oddball appliances bought suddenly

On impulse, which we'll likely never use;
Books we might read someday, to teach us skills
We'll really need because the daily news
predicts this trend or that will make our bills

go down if we learn how to do ourselves
what we pay others for. And the bookcase may
have given birth to propped-up dusty shelves
leaned on the wall in our cluttered hallway.

Then there's the junk we can't bear to let go.
We might need it if, well — you never know.

THE LEGACY

I own a house where I don't feel at home,
Left to me by a relative now dead,
Where mouths would rarely kiss but often foam,
And all seemed black and white when we saw red;
Where tenderness would always have its price;
Resentment would go hand in hand with love;
And each mistake we made would turn to ice,
Reminding us no good was good enough;
With walls not just around, but in between;
With windows curtained off against the sun;
Yet every tiny nuance would be seen,
And noted like one more debt left undone.
I am the king there now; tight is my crown.
If not for neighbors, I would burn it down.

THE SPELL OF THE RUINS

Here stand the crumbling remnants of a wall.
A long-demolished roof lets in the sky.
Decapitated statues standing by
Once served as sentries till they gave their all

To whatever the place stood for. Recall?
No one who can remains alive. So why
Can we still sense some power here? Don't try
To dodge the shadows that still fall.

To look at these remains, replace the lack
With what imaginations recognize.
We all know how it was, though how we know

Remains a mystery our minds attack
Without enthusiasm. Close your eyes
And let all your defenses go.

THE SURREALISTS

They made their way along the narrow ledge,
Afraid to fall, but with a goal in sight.
Beyond it was a cave in which the edge
Between this world and that glowed blue and bright.

To leave behind the everyday domain
Where all they had were things they'd settled for;
In search of driving horizontal rain
To wash away the gaudy paint they wore —

All this, they had in mind before they stepped
Too carelessly to see the now and here.
One fell, reached out for help, and so he kept
His young companion with him in his fear.

They plummeted, devoured by the abyss.
The world droned on, like nothing was amiss.

TOOKIE

Stanley "Tookie" Williams, died December 13, 2005

    Crips gang founder/anti-gang author Stanley "Tookie" Williams was executed at San Quentin for four murders committed during two 1979 hold-ups. Though demonstrators, some of them famous, gathered outside to protest his death, California Governor Arnold Schwarzenegger denied Williams clemency because he maintained his innocence and would not confess to his crimes. The lethal injection took an unusually long time to administer because Williams' arm was too muscular for the needle to be easily inserted.

The man convicted of multiple deaths
Had arms too muscular to let the needle in.
His body was too strong to just quit breath —
No matter if his soul were stained with sin.

Supporters sang and carried signs outside;
He had become a death row cause celeb.
Both Hollywood and victims' loved ones cried
Against and for his death's collected debt.

To the end, the crimes he never would confess
Would drive the governor to flex his muscles too.
Tension between the men became a test
Of which deserved the louder ballyhoo.

The inmate's veins at last gave up his ghost.
To whose strength should we raise a glass and toast?

FRIENDLY WITH DEATH

You tell yourself the leopard is a pet.
You raised her since she was a cub. She'll purr,
Roll over on her back, and offer her
Belly for rubbing. Sometimes, she will let

You kiss her forehead; then she'll lick your face.
Her black fur, soft and sleek, her yellow eyes
That shine like night-lights as in bed she lies
Beside you — such a vision to embrace

Intoxicates you like expensive booze.
You trust, if there were trouble, she would claw
Off an intruder's face to save you. Awe
Remains in you, of course, but when the news

Reports another death, you turn away.
You live in drunken love from day to day.

DEAD SILENCE

No reason to be jealous of the dead,
Although we're told they're "in a better place;"
We're told they're "at peace," or reunited
With the loved ones they have lost. The hard pace

Of life no longer wears on them. Maybe
If you believe they'll reincarnate, that
Last platitude collapses. Mystery
Is all we really know, however, at

The limits of our own experience.
We may long to rush into a white light
Within which we'll be cleansed of all torments,
No matter how persistently they bite.

But we don't know, even if we believe
In séances and such. And we must grieve.

SOMETHING SENSED ON SAMHAIN

Tonight, the veil between the worlds is thin,
Between this world and that — this, and the next.
A kind of overhearing ushers in
Awareness of dim things no one detects
On ordinary days. Fall falls away.
Winter's cold fingertips first find the spine.
We shudder when we sense the edges fray
Between present and past. Voices remind
Us of old conversations gone
From all but memory most of the year.
Tonight, it's more than echo going on.
Even what went unsaid may brush the ear.
The path may seem to end; everyday eyes
Won't follow where it leads. But nothing dies.

A SHOPPING MALL SANTA'S CHRISTMAS EVE

An ornamented tree cut from its roots
Stands slowly dying in the living room.
Beside it, on some newspaper, black boots
Dry off, reflect the twinkling lights that loom
Above, strung loosely bough to bough.
Bourbon sloshes in a tired man's glass,
To ease the tremors in hands empty now
Of greasy green bills making a quick pass.
To wealth and health he's never known, he drinks,
Aware he celebrates an irony.
He knows his children aren't where he thinks
On this night, at this late hour, they should be.
His wife despises him. His work is done.
But this is the worst time of year to run.

UNRESOLVED

In this, my New Year's Eve delirium,
I treasure every loss that's haunted me;
I savor each mistake that struck friends dumb,
Excuses executed brilliantly.
Some unpaid debts my mind can't even name
Gnaw angrily at inner cellar walls.
A smoking pocket of forgotten blame
Blind to its target clicks, chokes and forestalls.

It is a night for vows. I'll write a list.
I peer through steamy windows at pure dark.
Beyond my walls, an unforgiving mist
Of blown snow goes on burying the park.
It drifts. My fingers drum, then make a fist
Around my pen which moves, but leaves no mark.

THE FIRST SYMPTOMS
OF THE NEW YEAR

The pains we carry with us from last year
Throb quietly despite balms we apply.
Our own reflection, red-eyed, mystified,
Regards us with a subtle hint of fear,

Bewildered by recurrent punishment.
We don't know how or why we hurt ourselves.
We only know that certain things ring bells
In us, make our insistent guilt angels relent,

And we absorb some poison that lets us
Let go. Ironic that what turns down pain
Allows pleasant sensations a free reign,
Albeit temporarily. We trust

At last, in comforts that will quickly fade.
Though aching, we'll join the new year's parade.

VARIETIES OF DANGER

The sidewalk gleams with grains of broken glass.
Even in sandals, you can cut your foot.
The woods may serve up stings, and even put
Snakes in your path, hidden and toxic, as

A test of your alertness. But you pass
The city limits with more fear. It's not
Some animal that terrifies you, but
The human predators. You haul your ass

In certain neighborhoods, where you believe
The hunger is the worst. But hunger hunts
The prosperous; locks and alarms attract

The challenged; so-called "security" may leave
A lot to some imaginations; wants
Hurt worse than steps on a copperhead's back.

WILD RABBITS

They live in peace behind the restaurant.
The zoning keeps out guns that cut life short.
The grass grows, and in sunlight they cavort
And multiply however much they want.

Only a hawk or cat would be so blunt
As to ignore laws human folks must sort
Through to stay nameless in a crime report.
So long ears perk up. Swoop or pounce may haunt

Their huddled dreams, although they burrow deep
In what the meek inherit. Philosophy
Is only for the caged. Though cats may creep,

They go home for their meals. If you'd be free,
Part of it is a dance with danger. So
Patrons call it "wildlife" that they see.

HUNTER

Hawk perches on a pole as cars hiss by,
Imagining the sudden taste of blood,
The sound of tearing flesh, the tasty eye
Plucked by his beak before the heart's last thud.

Hawk's mind is not on cruelty, but on love;
Love of the senses flooded by the kill.
His victims are not real to him; above
It all, buoyed by a hungry thrill,

And so he will go soaring, peering down
On objects seen so small from such great height —
No closeness but in conquest, when the pound
Of some small heart could strengthen his delight.

They only lived a moment in his head —
Mere dots on a flat map, until he fed.

SCARECROW

The birds, who can't appreciate the art,
Peck at his propped-up sleeves, perch on his hat.
His face is painted on a burlap sack,
Angry enough to cause a heart attack

But only to an old, old man whose brain
Is addled by his age. A length of chain
Hangs from his waist, a sort of belt; in back,
You see how bent nails hold him up. You'd hack

If you had allergies to hay, the stuff
That substitutes for flesh, but otherwise,
He'll pose no threat. The ones who made him put

No fear in him: no thoughts of evil eyes
That watched from underneath the bed; no rough
Voice calling in the dark; no drop of blood.

PURROGATIVE

A cat decides the terms of where and when
Love is allowed expression, and of how.
To pet or scratch or rub the belly, then,
Are pointless should the cat decide, "not now."

You have a catlike grace, and when you bend,
You're in the mood to bend. You never bow
To anyone's idea of a friend
Or lover's duty. Should your mood allow

An open moment, or a warm caress,
What you accept is also what you give.
The privilege of loving you is best

Reserved for moments when you might forgive
Fragility in me, and not feel pressed.
I wait for your clear signal. Then I live.

TOWARD TWILIGHT

The agitated air grabs at your hat
And so do you, to keep from giving chase.
A leather jacket holds your warmth in place,
As you run errands, tend to this and that.

The sun will soon be gone. The shadows, flat
Now, will envelop the whole place.
For now, the sense of safety we embrace
Comforts the runner and the sleepy cat

Stretched out on someone's windowsill. You pat
Your pocket to make sure steel rings encase
The keys you need to enter what safe space
You call your own, though you just rent your little flat.

Dusk settles. The cat goes out on the prowl.
Somewhere nearby, you hear an untamed howl.

NIGHT BLOOMING

The deer come out to graze when the sun sets.
The whole herd fills the meadow at the edge
Of town, and we observe an etiquette
Of sorts; from a respectful distance, pledge

To come no closer, silently. One young
Buck keeps his head up, keeps his eyes on us.
The rest munch grass as if we weren't there. Hung
Low, the other's heads appear at rest. "Trust

In your hunger, it will tell the time,"
They seem to say, with their mouths full. You take
My hand in yours; no one sees but the buck.
No hunters here to sneer at the sublime.

Night is the time some blossoms open, so
We leave this scene. To our warm place we go.

THE GREEN MAN

An image in the ornate metal grate
That guards the cellar window from kicked stones
Betrays a man's face, gazing as he waits,
Hidden among the leaves, silent, alone,

Where no one notices, presumes to judge
His motives. He remains mysterious.
From this safe vantage point, he'll never budge;
Frozen forever in his role as just

Observer — conscious, but uncivilized.
Amid his camouflage of vegetation
He can be a face with penetrating eyes
That don't betray his quiet cogitation.

Society thinks he's been left behind.
He smiles and keeps the secrets of his mind.

JAPANESE SONNET

A stream between two
Green slopes. Ducks float; the current
Carries them along,

Effortless. The blue
Flowers on the bank weren't
There last week. Fish throng

Under the clear view;
Silver flashes only lent
To eyes — blink; they're gone.

The sun reaches through
Early spring chill, intent
On making colors strong.

All things, moving at their pace,
Bring this moment to this place.

YES, WHITMAN WROTE NO SONNETS, BUT...

1. Walt Whitman in Modern Manhattan

I am a turnstile through which thousands pass:
That's just the kind of thing that Walt would say,
If only he were here with us today.
The hordes that flow through this station would blast

Even Walt's senses. Though he loved big crowds,
He never saw mobs like we daily see —
The products of the breeding factory
That makes this place teem like an anthill. Loud

Hiss of subway doors, hundreds of rushing feet,
The madness of the normal morning rush —
It would thud through him, tidal wave to flush
His brain. I'd lead him to the raucous street,

And watch the wonder in his boggled eyes,
And wait for what he'd say in his surprise.

2. An Imagined Contemporary Sonnet By Walt Whitman

I am a turnstile through which thousands pass.
I stand upon the threshold of their daily journey.
The workers rush through me, to steel and glass
Skyscraper destinations — how can we

Live at such a pace as this? Pete's streetcar
Never hurtled through such tunnels underground.
It travels in a blink where once was far.
One must scream to be heard above such sound.

What I imagined was warm to my touch.
The smell and taste and feel of the embrace
Were as I'd dreamed. I relished them so much,
I wished such joy for all men everyplace.

I understand there is more freedom now —
As much, they say, as time and space allow.

HAIKU & SENRYU

caterpillar creeps
along the branch as dusk comes
silk sleep, flying dreams

hawk stands on brown grass
weary of an empty sky
no sign of squirrels

lights blink on the lawn
firefly evangelism
crickets testify

ants build a sand hill
feverish effort of mob
a fragile castle

wide green eyes, long claws,
but the butterfly's too quick —
one frustrated cat

caterpillar crawls
across the highway slowly
and yet he survives

ducks in parking lot
popcorn on the grass island
left by the lonely

      groundhogs on roadside
      stand on hind legs, stare at cars
      poised as if to wave

            crow perched on bronze head
            statue has gone green in rain
            dung on hero's face

path by the river
sweat catches sun on bare chest
man jogs memory

      milk carton snapshots
      someone's missing children
      carefree expressions

            blue water, green grass
            passers-by chatting in Greek
            paddleboat tourists

ever greyer sky
wind swaying budding branches
storm gathers its force

    no cat in window
    thunder drives her downstairs
    noise clouds her judgment

        sky darkens at noon,
        but though the sun has vanished —
        sudden flash of light

wind yanks umbrella
struggle with books under arm
poetry gets wet

    cop's raised palm halts cars
    big grey turtle crosses road
    drivers wait, grinning

        head propped on turtle
        belly on log, tail in stream
        alligator dreams

squirrel on the bar
begs nuts from half-drunk tourists
till flashbulb startles

naked man in tree
police take their time coming
small town Saturday

crane knee deep in stream
drinks, calm, though people watch him
till camera clicks

hurricane coming
breakers way too big to surf
FOR SALE sign floats by

brown rabbit, steel cage
clear inverted bottle drips
dream of green meadow

stiff yellow-brown grass
silent gasp of bone-dry creek
summer without ducks

silver crescent moon
visible in afternoon
leaves ready to fall

    train screams in the night
    carnations tremble in vase
    cat's ears rise in sleep

        raising the hatchet
        arthritis signals autumn
        man winces, log splits

chipmunk's reddish blur
darts across front step and gone
effort not to blink

    hungry squirrel leaps
    from roof peak to maple branch
    much like Monkey Mind

        streaks low to the ground,
        black and white blur — a cat?
        skunk crosses the street

geese wintering North
too fat from lack of flying
rule Riverfront Park

      statue of Kwannon
      flowers, water, incense, fruit
      light candle, bow head

           a lone rose, dying
           in a vase — no worse anguish
           in the universe

FIXED FORMS USED IN THIS BOOK

Form	Poems
Ballade	Survivor Story
Burns Stanza	Red Eye
Haiku	Nature poems in *Haiku And Senryu*
Limerick (as stanza form)	The Saga of Bob
Pantoum	Desk Job
	Things We Forget
Quatern	Ways of Life
Rondeau	Real Man Rondeau
	Sparring Partners
	Fathers and Sons
Senryu	Poems about people in *Haiku And Senryu* & stanzas in Men's Room Senryu
Sestina	And Then Time Moves
Sonnet	All poems in *Sonnets* except Japanese Sonnet, which combines elements of Haiku, Tanka & the Sonnet
Sonnet (as stanza form)	The Affair (a crown of sonnets)
Tanka (as stanza form)	"It"
Terza Rima (as stanza form)	Kinetic
Triolet	Hunger For Things Not Canned
Triolet (as stanza form)	X And Y
Villanelle	A Holiday
	Control: A Rationale
	Do Not Go Gentle, Just *Go*
	Turnabout
	A Blind Date With Phil Spector
	Visiting Hours
	Widow's Hill

NOTES ON POEMS

WAYS OF LIFE
Lynn Loomis was my psychotherapist for many years. The refrain line "Everybody starts from where they are" is something she said to me in a session that stuck with me.

THE SAGA OF BOB
I refer to "God's sixth command" in this poem because I was brought up Catholic, and Catholics follow the order for the ten commandments given by Augustine of Hippo. Augustine's order lists the sixth commandment as "Thou shalt not commit adultery." This differs from the order given in Judaism, and the order given by Origen of Alexandria, which most Protestants follow. (Both of these say the sixth commandment is "'Thou shalt not kill.")

By the way, the character Bob is a composite, not one actual person. Several people at readings have told me that he reminds them of someone they know, so I figured I'd better clear that up before I get sued.

HUNGER FOR THINGS NOT CANNED
A triolet in honor of our late cat Speedy, who we let go outside because her previous owners had, and there was no keeping her in. It was written while she was still very much alive and on the prowl. We lost her when she was run down by a car.

JADED
"More! More! More!" is a 1976 dance hit by the Andrea True Connection. Andrea True was a former porno star.

COMPELLED
Describes habitual drugged cruising at the Club Baths and similar places in the early 70s, before we knew about the HIV virus.

X AND Y
This apparently mysterious title is a simple pun on "Ex" and "Why."

KINETIC
This one is about mind-over-matter phenomena such as telekinesis and pyrokinesis, familiar from such popular Stephen King novels as *Carrie* and *Firestarter*. "Wild talents" was a phrase coined by Charles Fort to describe such abilities, and the title of his 1933 speculative nonfiction book on the subject.

NEIGHBORS
"Neighbors" is about a serial killer like John Wayne Gacy, but not any one of them in particular.

A BLIND DATE WITH PHIL SPECTOR
The legendary producer of pop hits by such girl groups as The Ronettes and The Crystals is notorious for his "allegedly" reckless behavior with guns and his "alleged" abuse of women, but always found female companionship. He was convicted of the 1999 shooting death of actress Lana Clarkson in 2009 and is now in prison.

SPIRIT ANTHEM
I wrote "Spirit Anthem" to the tune of a contemporary Christian hymn at the request of my life partner, Dave Walker, who was then conducting the choir at a Unitarian Church. He liked the tune and wanted me to give it appropriate words for that liberal congregation to sing. Ultimately it was never performed by the choir except in rehearsal. It turns out that at around the same time, the pastor had written a bland unrhymed lyric that was set to music by another chorister, with the intention of having it performed by the choir and an orchestra at a large regional church meeting at a local art center, but my partner and I were not immediately made privy to that information. Our addition of "Spirit Anthem" to the group's repertoire was postponed indefinitely, and we were told it was because the hymn's music was "too hard" for the choir to learn — though the music for the pastor's lyric was "classical," much more sophisticated, and had to be learned in a fairly short time, and though (more glaringly) the choir already knew "Spirit Anthem." We no longer attend this church.

WIDOW'S HILL
Widow's Hill is the name of a seaside cliff in the 1960s Gothic soap opera "Dark Shadows," notorious in fictional Collinsport, Maine as the site where wives would mourn sailor husbands lost at sea. It was also the site of the suicide of major series character Josette DuPree, bride-to-be of cursed protagonist Barnabas Collins.

LAST TOAST TO POE
In 2009 I and a group of poets from the Harrisburg, PA area seriously discussed going to Baltimore to visit Edgar Allan Poe's grave on his birthday, January 19. An unknown person known as "The Poe Toaster" had been leaving roses and a bottle of cognac on Poe's grave sometime during that night since 1949. Our excursion never happened — but that was also the first night in 60 years when the tradition was not carried out. We're pretty sure the "Poe Toaster" wasn't one of our number, though.

SORRY, EMILY DICKINSON
It's a familiar joke among poets that most of Emily Dickinson's poems can be sung to the tune of "The Yellow Rose of Texas." So can this poem. I've been accused of ridiculing Dickinson with this poem, and I don't mean to; the older I get, the more I empathize with her withdrawal from society. The title is not meant as an apology for the poem, but for how poorly Dickinson was understood during her lifetime, even by the people who supported her. I admire her for handling this with such characteristic humility.

WHEN I MET GWENDOLYN BROOKS
In 1990, the Pennsylvania Council on the Arts sent me to work for six months as a publicist for the African American Historical And Cultural Museum in Philadelphia. For me, the highlight of this experience was sitting beside the very gracious Gwendolyn Brooks, making change while she signed just-sold copies of her collection *Blacks*. I'm very grateful that I had the honor and thrill of meeting this great poet while she was still with us.

EPITAPH FOR QUENTIN
I had the honor of interviewing the late Quentin Crisp twice during my career as a journalist, and the pleasure of having dinner with him on a couple of other occasions. Among several other books, Quentin wrote the famous autobiography *The Naked Civil Servant*, and was played by John Hurt in the critically acclaimed British television film based on it. He was a sweet man who constantly said very quotable things, and who had an unusual philosophy of life that made a great deal of sense to me. Because of this philosophical bent and penchant for aphorism, I once said in an article that Quentin was the gay equivalent of a Lao Tzu or Confucius. I could start a religion based on his ideas, but he probably wouldn't have approved of that (although he'd probably also have been too polite to say so). Still, "Crispianity" has a nice ring to it, don't you think?

THE AFFAIR
This series of sonnets describes a young gay man's ultimately painful clandestine relationship with an older married guy. Not that I'd personally know anything about such ill-advised behavior.

SUPPORT
The sonnet "Support" describes how my partner Dave kept me company before and after I had surgery at Milton Hershey Medical Center. The poem first appeared in the Medical Center's literary magazine.

A QUIET MEMORY
… is set in Atlantic City, NJ, in the early 1960s.

FINAL GIRL
"Final Girl" is how fans and critics refer to the obligatory female sole survivor in a slasher film.

TOOKIE
The spelling of the word "celeb" is deliberate — a play on words. The facts on Tookie and some of his story are on the same page as the poem. For the record, let me say that I am against the death penalty for anyone, ever. But I got the idea for the poem from the fact that Tookie and Arnold Schwarzenegger, who signed his death warrant, were both bodybuilders, and the musculature of Tookie's arm resisted the lethal injection and delayed his execution. I found this bitterly ironic.

YES, WHITMAN WROTE NO SONNETS, BUT…
The name "Pete" refers to Peter Doyle, Walt Whitman's longtime companion, who was working as a streetcar conductor when he and Walt first met.

HAIKU AND SENRYU
"Monkey Mind" is a Buddhist term that refers to the chaotic, easily distracted state of mind that most Westerners consider "normal." "Kwannon" is the Japanese name for Kuan Yin, the Chinese goddess of compassion. Her name means "She Who Hears the Cries of the World." Among other things, she is a patron of the abused.

ABOUT THE POET

A 2010 nominee for a Pushcart Prize, Jack Veasey is a Philadelphia native who has been living in Hummelstown, PA for over 20 years. He is the author of ten previous published collections of poetry, most recently *The Sonnets* and *5-7-5* (both from Small Hours Press, 2007).

His poems have also appeared in many periodicals including *Christopher Street, The Pittsburgh Quarterly, Assaracus, Harbinger: A Journal of Social Ecology, The Philadelphia Daily News, The Painted Bride Quarterly, Fledgling Rag, Oxalis, The Blue Guitar, Bone and Flesh, Zone: A Feminist Journal for Women and Men, Film Library Quarterly* (Museum of Modern Art, NYC), *Experimental Forest, Tabula Rasa, Wild Onions, Mouth of the Dragon, Asphodel, Insight, The Irish Edition, The Harrisburg Patriot-News, The Harrisburg Review, The Princeton Spectrum, The Little Word Machine (UK)*, and *The Body Politic (Canada)*, among others. His poems have also appeared in a number of anthologies, including *Common Wealth: Contemporary Poets On Pennsylvania* (Penn State University Press), *Sweet Jesus: Poems About The Ultimate Icon* (Anthology Press, Los Angeles), and *A Loving Testimony: Remembering Loved Ones Lost To AIDS* (The Crossing Press, Freedom, CA).

His plays have been produced by Theater Center Philadelphia and Theater of the Seventh Sister (Lancaster, PA). He has hosted literary radio programs for WITF FM in Harrisburg and WXPN FM in Philadelphia. He was awarded a Fellowship from the PA Council On The Arts and is a two-time honoree of The PA Center for the Book's PENNBOOK celebration. For many years he hosted poetry readings in the Harrisburg area at The Art Association of Harrisburg's Paper Sword series and at Encore Books and Music, Borders Books and Music, and Open Stage of Harrisburg, and also taught poetry writing courses at Harrisburg Area Community College Community Education Center, Martin Memorial Library in York, and for the Dauphin County Library System. He is a member of Harrisburg's notorious (Almost) Uptown Poetry Cartel.

Veasey spent the seventies and eighties working as a journalist for such publications as *The Philadelphia Inquirer, Philadelphia Magazine, Pennsylvania Magazine, APPRISE, The Philadelphia City Paper*, and *The Cherry Hill Courier Post*, and editing a number of periodicals in Philadelphia and New York, including *The South Street Star, The Philadelphia Gay News*, and *FirstHand Magazine*. His articles for the *Philadelphia Gay News* won two awards from the national Lesbian and Gay Press Association. He recently wrote an article on Walt Whitman's relationship with his longtime companion Peter Doyle that was syndicated to 40 periodicals nationwide by the Gay History Project, followed by another article about Whitman's involvement in the United States Civil War.

A singer as well as a poet, Veasey has released one CD album of original songs, "Build A Fire," as lead singer of the folk-rock duo Open Book. In 2010, Veasey released a CD single of another original song, "Whether or Not the World Knows." He sings second tenor with the Harrisburg Gay Men's Chorus. He has been with his partner in life, David Walker, since 1978.

ABOUT THIS BOOK

The body text of this book is set in Aldine type, a face inspired by the designs of the great humanist printer and publisher Aldus Manutius.

Headlines are set in Aldine, and smaller headlines and poem titles in Futura, a Bauhaus-influenced type that came to be one of the most popular sans-serif faces of the 20th century. Its geometric emphasis and even width of stroke takes its form from classic Greek column lettering, but looks completely modern because of its strict use of geometric forms (circles and isosceles triangles). The hot metal face was designed in 1927 for the Bauer foundry in Germany.

The digital art used for the cover, title-page and section titles are all derived from a digital photo by Brett Rutherford.

www.ingramcontent.com/pod-product-compliance
Lightning Source LLC
Chambersburg PA
CBHW051654040426
42446CB00009B/1130